EARTH SCIENCE—LANDFORMS Need to Know

SilverTip

Mountains and Cliffs

by Ashley Kuehl

Consultant: Jordan Stoleru,
Science Educator

BEARPORT
PUBLISHING

Minneapolis, Minnesota

Credits

Cover and title page, © Nathaniel Gonzales/iStock; 3, © Ruslan Suseynov/Shutterstock; 4–5, © krissanapongw/iStock; 6–7, © Kemter/iStock; 9, © Daniel Prudek/Shutterstock; 10, © Jess Kraft/Shutterstock; 11, © Marco Ritzki/Shutterstock; 13, © Ron and Patty Thomas/iStock; 14, © Vixit/Shutterstock; 14–15, © Josef Pittner/Shutterstock; 17, © asmithers/iStock; 18, © Trphotos/Shutterstock; 19, © RudolfT/iStock Photo; 21, © Christian Colista/Shutterstock; 22–23, © Michael Andrew Just/Shutterstock; 25, © Alex Potemkin/iStock; 27, © prochasson frederic/Shutterstock; 28, © Ozant/Shutterstock.

Bearport Publishing Company Product Development Team

President: Jen Jenson; Director of Product Development: Spencer Brinker; Managing Editor: Allison Juda; Associate Editor: Naomi Reich; Associate Editor: Tiana Tran; Art Director: Colin O'Dea; Designer: Kim Jones; Designer: Kayla Eggert; Product Development Assistant: Owen Hamlin

Statement on Usage of Generative Artificial Intelligence

Bearport Publishing remains committed to publishing high-quality nonfiction books. Therefore, we restrict the use of generative AI to ensure accuracy of all text and visual components pertaining to a book's subject. See BearportPublishing.com for details.

Library of Congress Cataloging-in-Publication Data

Names: Kuehl, Ashley, 1977– author.
Title: Mountains and cliffs / By Ashley Kuehl.
Description: Minneapolis, Minnesota : Bearport Publishing Company, [2025] | Series: Earth science-landforms: need to know | Includes bibliographical references and index.
Identifiers: LCCN 2023059663 (print) | LCCN 2023059664 (ebook) | ISBN 9798892320504 (library binding) | ISBN 9798892325240 (paperback) | ISBN 9798892321839 (ebook)
Subjects: LCSH: Mountains–Juvenile literature. | Cliffs–Juvenile literature.
Classification: LCC GB512 .K84 2025 (print) | LCC GB512 (ebook) | DDC 551.43/2–dc23/eng/20240104
LC record available at https://lccn.loc.gov/2023059663
LC ebook record available at https://lccn.loc.gov/2023059664

Copyright © 2025 Bearport Publishing Company. All rights reserved. No part of this publication may be reproduced in whole or in part, stored in any retrieval system, or transmitted in any form or by any means, electronic, mechanical, photocopying, recording, or otherwise, without written permission from the publisher. Bearport Publishing is a division of Chrysalis Education Group.

For more information, write to Bearport Publishing, 5357 Penn Avenue South, Minneapolis, MN 55419.

Contents

Tall and Steep. 4

Mighty Mountains. 6

How Mountains Form 8

Growing and Shrinking. 12

Steep Walls of Rock 16

Creating a Cliff 18

Constantly Changing 20

How's the Weather up There? 24

Moving and Changing. 26

Tectonic Plates Make Mountains. 28

SilverTips for Success 29

Glossary 30

Read More 31

Learn More Online 31

Index 32

About the Author. 32

Tall and Steep

Some parts of Earth rise high above the rest of the land. Mountains can be so tall that their tops are hidden by clouds. Cliffs are high, too. These steep walls of rock tower over crashing water or deep valleys. What do you know about these tall **landforms**?

Landforms are features on Earth's surface. They can be many shapes and sizes. Mountains, cliffs, hills, and valleys are all landforms.

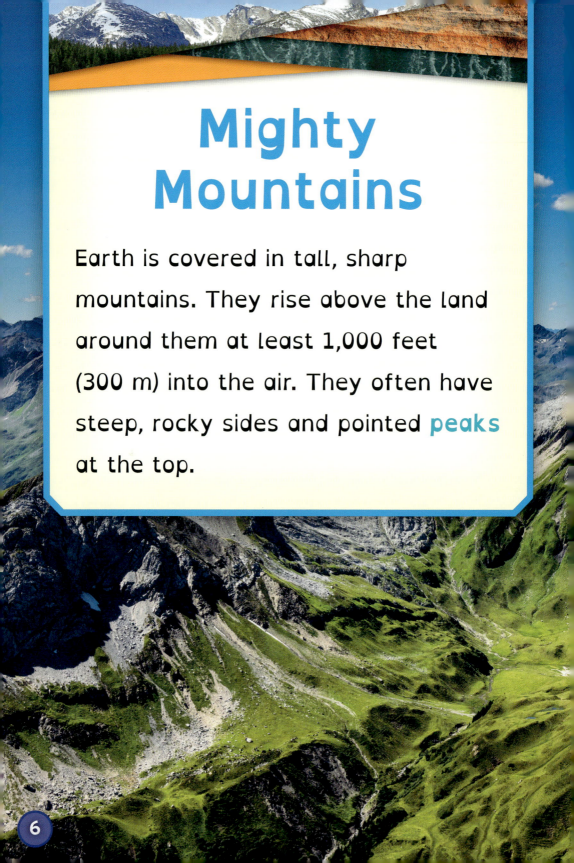

Mighty Mountains

Earth is covered in tall, sharp mountains. They rise above the land around them at least 1,000 feet (300 m) into the air. They often have steep, rocky sides and pointed **peaks** at the top.

Mountains are usually found in groups. A series of mountains is called a **range**. Some ranges are quite long. The Alps chain of mountains stretches about 750 miles (1,200 km) across Europe.

How Mountains Form

Mountains can form in a few ways. Often, they start with action underground. Earth's crust, or outer layer, is made of large, flat rocks. They are called **tectonic plates**.

These plates are always slowly moving. Sometimes, they bump into one another. This may push rocks and earth up into mountains.

As tectonic plates push together, the edge of one plate can slide over another. Or both plates can crunch together and push up. Both of these things can make mountains.

The Himalayas began forming when two tectonic plates smashed together.

Some mountains pile up at Earth's surface. Superhot liquid rock called **magma** flows beneath the tectonic plates. Sometimes, it pushes up to the surface through cracks called volcanoes. The hot rock cools above ground, hardening into solid rock. If enough rock builds up, it can form a mountain.

Magma can build up underground, too. As it does, it can push land up from below, making mountains. The Black Hills in South Dakota were formed in this way.

Once magma is above ground it is called lava.

Growing and Shrinking

Mountains form over thousands or even millions of years. But they never stop changing. Earth's tectonic plates keep moving. This makes some mountains grow even taller. The Sierra Nevada mountain range in the western United States grows about half an inch (1.3 cm) every 10 years.

> The Sierra Nevada is growing relatively quickly. Scientists are studying why. They think the amount of water in the mountains might affect their height.

The Sierra Nevada mountain range

Mountains can also get flatter. Tectonic movement can make this happen from below. The rocks of mountains can wear away above ground, too.

Glaciers are huge sheets of ice that slowly travel across land. As they move, some glaciers break large pieces of rock off mountains.

Mount Everest is both growing and shrinking. Crashing tectonic plates push this huge mountain even taller. At the same time, wind and water are wearing away the rock!

Steep Walls of Rock

Cliffs are tall, rocky landforms that are usually smaller than mountains. Their steep walls are often found along coastlines. They sometimes form in the low areas between hills or mountains. Instead of the angled sides of mountains, cliffs often have an almost vertical drop-off.

The White Cliffs of Dover stretch along the coast of southeast England. They are about 14 miles (23 km) long. These cliffs are made of chalk, which is why they look white.

The White Cliffs of Dover

Creating a Cliff

Most cliffs are formed by weathering and erosion. Wind or water break apart bits of large rocks. This is called weathering. Then, the blowing winds or rushing water wash the bits away through erosion. Ocean waves break off and wash away lots of pieces of cliff walls, too.

Arches National Park in Utah has many cliffs. Wind and water shaped the rock over millions of years. It left behind arches.

Constantly Changing

Like all landforms, cliffs change over time. Weathering and erosion can make holes in a cliff wall. Sometimes, the holes grow into large caves.

Other times, the top or edge of a cliff can break off. Wind and flowing water are major causes of these breaks, too.

People have long built homes in cliff caves. About a thousand years ago, **Ancestral** Pueblo people lived in cave homes in what is now the southwest United States.

The kinds of rocks that cliffs are made of can impact their weathering and erosion. Soft rocks break apart more easily. Harder rocks tend to come apart in sharper pieces.

Cliffs made of softer rocks often become smoother. They are less steep. Cliffs of harder rocks become steep and jagged.

A cliff can have more than one kind of rock in it. As it weathers, softer rock breaks off more easily. That can make unusual shapes.

How's the Weather up There?

Weather shapes tall landforms, but mountains can also affect the weather! How? Storms often build up as winds hit a mountain. However, the system fizzles out before reaching the top. One side of the mountain may get lots of rain or snow. The other side stays dry.

Many mountains are so tall that different parts have different **climates**. A mountain's top might be cold and snowy. At the same time, the bottom can be warm and dry.

A rain shadow is a patch of land that is dry because a mountain blocks wet weather.

Moving and Changing

Mountains and cliffs have long shaped life on Earth. For millions of years, they have been moving and changing. They are still moving today, even if we can't see it. In a million years, Earth might have very different mountain ranges and cliffs.

The Rocky Mountains and Colorado Plateau looked different more than six million years ago. That's when scientists think the Colorado River started carving out rock, making the Grand Canyon.

Tectonic Plates Make Mountains

As tectonic plates move, one might slide under another.

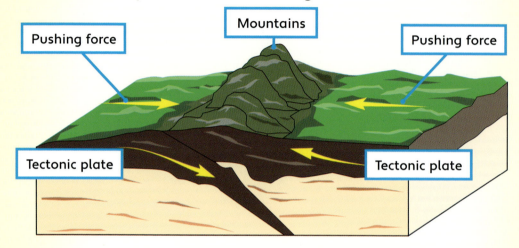

Two plates pushing against each other can make the land crumple and push up.

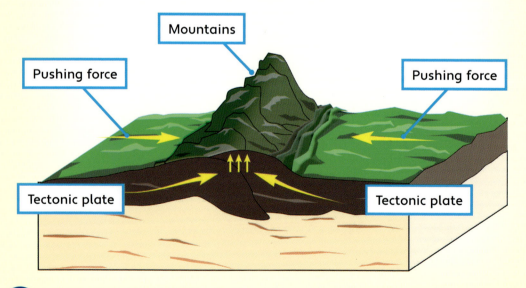

SilverTips for SUCCESS

★ SilverTips for REVIEW

Review what you've learned. Use the text to help you.

Define key terms

cliff
erosion
mountain
tectonic plates
weathering

Check for understanding

Explain how tectonic plates can change Earth's surface.

In what ways can magma make mountains?

How do weathering and erosion affect cliffs?

Think deeper

What is the surface of Earth like where you live? How does the land around you affect you?

★ SilverTips on TEST-TAKING

- **Make a study plan.** Ask your teacher what the test is going to cover. Then, set aside time to study a little bit every day.

- **Read all the questions carefully.** Be sure you know what is being asked.

- **Skip any questions** you don't know how to answer right away. Mark them and come back later if you have time.

Glossary

ancestral having to do with family members who lived long ago

climates typical weather patterns in various places

erosion the carrying away of rock and soil by natural forces, such as water and wind

jagged having a sharp or uneven surface

landforms natural features on Earth's surface

magma hot melted rock found beneath Earth's surface

peaks the pointed tops of mountains

range a set of mountains that form a group

tectonic plates huge pieces of rock that make up Earth's outer crust

weathering the breaking apart or wearing away of rock and soil by natural forces, such as water and wind

Read More

Bowman, Chris. *Great Smoky Mountains National Park (U.S. National Parks).* Minneapolis: Bellwether Media, 2023.

Owen, Ruth. *Sedimentary Rocks (Earth Science–Geology: Need to Know).* Minneapolis: Bearport Publishing Company, 2022.

Romero, Libby. *All about Volcanoes: Discovering How Earth Erupts (A True Book: Natural Disaster!).* New York: Children's Press, 2021.

Learn More Online

1. Go to **www.factsurfer.com** or scan the QR code below.
2. Enter "**Mountains and Cliffs**" into the search box.
3. Click on the cover of this book to see a list of websites.

Index

caves 20

climate 24

crust 8, 10

erosion 18, 20, 22

glaciers 14

magma 10–11

peaks 6

ranges 7, 9, 12–13, 26

mountain ranges 8, 18

tectonic plates 8–10, 12, 14, 28

volcanoes 10

water 4, 12, 14, 18, 20

weather 24–25

weathering 18, 20, 22–23

wind 14, 18, 20, 24

About the Author

Ashley Kuehl is an editor and writer specializing in nonfiction for young people. She lives in Minneapolis, MN.